GETTING TO KNOW THE WORLD'S GREATEST ARTISTS

FAITH
RINGGOLD

WRITTEN AND ILLUSTRATED BY MIKE VENEZIA

FOUNTAINDALE PUBLIC LIBRARY

300 West Briarcliff Road
Bolingbrook, IL 60440-2894
(630)   759-2102

CHILDREN'S PRESS
AN IMPRINT OF SCHOLASTIC INC.
NEW YORK TORONTO LONDON AUCKLAND SYDNEY
MEXICO CITY NEW DELHI HONG KONG
DANBURY, CONNECTICUT

For Faith - Thanks for your help and inspiration, and reminding me that anyone can fly.

Cover: *Jazz Stories 2004: Mama Can Sing, Papa Can Blow #3: Gonna Get On Away from You,* by Faith Ringgold. 2004, acrylic on canvas with pieced border, 81 x 66 in. ACA Galleries, New York. Photo by Gamma One.

Colorist for illustrations: Andrew Day

Library of Congress Cataloging-in-Publication Data

Venezia, Mike.
   Faith Ringgold / written and illustrated by Mike Venezia.
     p. cm. — (Getting to know the world's greatest artists)
   ISBN-13: 978-0-531-18526-1 (lib. bdg.) 978-0-531-14757-3 (pbk.)
   ISBN-10: 0-531-18526-5 (lib. bdg.)   0-531-14757-6 (pbk.)
   1. Ringgold, Faith—Juvenile literature. 2. Artists—United
States—Biography—Juvenile literature. 3. African American
artists—Biography—Juvenile literature. I. Title. II. Series.

   N6537.R55V46 2008
   709.2—dc22
   [B]
                        2007016125

1 2 3 4 5 6 7 8 9 10 R 17 16 15 14 13 12 11 10 09 08

Photograph of Faith Ringgold in front of her story quilt *Tar Beach 2*
© Kathy Willens/AP Photo

Faith Ringgold was born in New York City in 1930. She grew up during a time of a lot of prejudice and discrimination in the United States. When she became a professional artist, Faith fought hard to make sure that African American artists received the attention and respect they deserved.

The Black Light Series: US America Black, by Faith Ringgold. 1969, oil on canvas, 60 x 84 in. Collection of the artist. Photograph courtesy Faith Ringgold.

Mrs. Brown and her Three Children: Catherine, Elsie and Dolores, by Faith Ringgold. 1973, mixed media. Collection of the artist. Photograph courtesy Faith Ringgold.

Faith Ringgold is known for her paintings, prints, masks, and soft sculptures. These works of art often show her feelings about being an African American woman. Faith's most famous works are her story quilts. Faith makes the quilts by sewing together painted canvas and quilted fabric. Then she adds handwritten stories.

Detail from *Who's Afraid of Aunt Jemima?* by Faith Ringgold. 1983, acrylic on canvas, dyed, painted and pieced fabric, 90 x 80 in. Private Collection. Photograph courtesy Faith Ringgold.

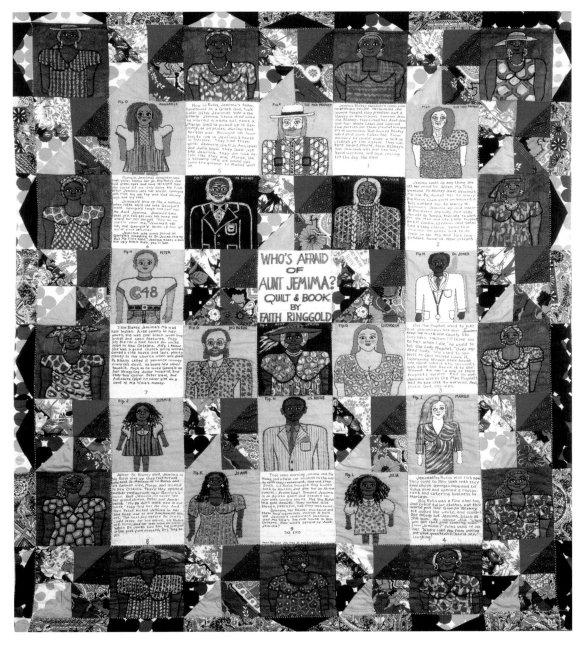

Who's Afraid of Aunt Jemima? by Faith Ringgold. 1983, acrylic on canvas, dyed, painted and pieced fabric, 90 x 80 in. Private Collection. Photograph courtesy Faith Ringgold.

With Faith's story quilts, you get to see great pictures and read about them at the same time.

Faith Ringgold, who was born Faith Jones, grew up in a section of New York City called Harlem. In the early 1900s, thousands of African Americans from southern states had moved to Harlem to find jobs and a better life. Many great jazz musicians, singers, athletes, authors, and artists lived in Harlem during the 1930s.

On hot summer nights, Faith's family and neighbors would go up to the roof of their apartment building to cool off. Because the roof was covered with tar paper, everyone called it Tar Beach. At night Faith loved to look up in the sky at all the stars.

Faith (left) at age six with her sister Barbara on the roof of their apartment in Harlem. Photograph courtesy Faith Ringgold.

Tar Beach, by Faith Ringgold. 1988, acrylic on canvas, tie-dyed, pieced fabric border, 74 x 69 in. Solomon R. Guggenheim Museum, New York. Photograph courtesy Faith Ringgold.

She could see her favorite bridge, the George Washington Bridge, all lit up. One of Faith's most famous story quilts is about the magic she felt on those hot summer evenings.

Faith (at right) with her sister Barbara and brother Andrew in 1938.
Photograph courtesy Faith Ringgold.

Storytelling was always an important part of Faith's life. When she was a little girl, Faith stayed up late listening to her parents, aunts, and uncles tell stories about their family history. Faith learned a lot and it was great fun.

Before people had television in their homes, storytelling and listening to the radio were major forms of entertainment. Faith and her brother and sister loved listening to radio shows. They let their imaginations run wild. When Faith was really little, she thought people were inside the radio talking through the speaker.

Faith spent a lot of her childhood at home. She was often sick with asthma. When Faith had an asthma attack, she had trouble breathing. During periods when Faith was sick, her mother, Willi, schooled her at home. Faith also spent lots of time drawing and coloring. Willi taught Faith to sew, too.

Faith made all kinds of neat things, like little shoes, purses, and even underwear! On days when Faith was feeling better, Willi would take her to museums and stage performances while her brother and sister were at school.

As a child, Faith was lucky enough to see live performances by such jazz greats as Duke Ellington (right) and Ella Fitzgerald (below).
Photograph of Duke Ellington © Corbis.

As an adult, Faith said she didn't remember much about her early school years. She would never forget the lively jazz shows she saw at the theater as a child, however. Jazz is an exciting style of music that was originated by African Americans. Faith thought the lively shows she saw were art, even more than paintings and sculptures were.

Jazz vocalist Ella Fitzgerald singing in the 1940s.
Photograph © Underwood & Underwood/Corbis.

Jazz Stories 2004: Mama Can Sing, Papa Can Blow #8: Don't Wanna Love You, by Faith Ringgold. 2004, acrylic on canvas with pieced border, 81 x 64 in. ACA Galleries, New York. Photograph courtesy Faith Ringgold.

Later, Faith would paint and make prints of jazz musicians and singers. These pictures are so colorful and full of life you can almost hear jazz music when you look at them!

Even though Faith was always interested in art, she didn't take any art classes in high school. She did practice at home, though. Faith often did portraits of friends and family members. When she went to the City College of New York, Faith studied education and art.

It was in college that Faith made up her mind to become a serious, full-time artist. One day, her instructor insulted a drawing she had made of a mountain scene. The instructor told Faith to label her mountains so he could tell what they were. He also told Faith he didn't think she had the talent to become an artist.

That was all Faith needed to hear! She
decided then and there to show her teacher
and everyone else she would be an artist.
A good one, too!

Michele, Faith, Willi, and Barbara (left to right) traveled to Europe by ship in 1961. Photograph courtesy Faith Ringgold.

During college, Faith married her high-school sweetheart, Earl Wallace. They had two daughters, Michele and Barbara. When Faith graduated, she got a job as an art teacher in a New York City public school. It wasn't an easy start for a young woman. To make matters worse, the marriage didn't work out. After four years, Faith and Earl separated.

Faith had to figure out how to raise two young daughters, work as an art teacher, continue her education, and find a way to become a full-time artist. Fortunately, Faith got a lot of help from her mom. Then, she fell in love with a man named Burdette Ringgold. Faith and Burdette got married in 1962.

Fishing Boats on a Beach, by Vincent van Gogh. 1888, oil on canvas, 25 1/2 x 32 in. © Art Resource/NY/ Van Gogh Museum, Amsterdam.

Female Head with Colored Hat, by Pablo Picasso. 1939, oil on canvas, 24 x 20 in. © Art Resource/NY/Nationalgalerie, Museum Berggruen, State Museum of Berlin, Germany.

Virgin and Child with St. Anne, by Leonardo da Vinci. c.1510, oil on panel, 66 x 44 in. © The Bridgeman Art Library/The Louvre, Paris.

Now that Faith had more help taking care of the girls, she really got busy working on her art. During her college years, Faith had learned about all the great European artists. Faith studied and copied the works of Vincent van Gogh, Pablo Picasso, and Leonardo da Vinci.

Provincetown #2, by Faith Ringgold. 1957, oil on board, 24 x 26 in. Collection of the artist.
Photograph courtesy Faith Ringgold.

Faith's first paintings were influenced by old master artists. Even though Faith appreciated and learned important lessons from European art, it really didn't seem to have much to do with her life or her experiences.

The American People Series #1: Between Friends, by Faith Ringgold. 1963, oil on canvas, 40 x 24 in. ACA Galleries, New York. Photograph courtesy Faith Ringgold.

Faith started doing paintings that were more meaningful to her. They were about things she saw going on in the United States at the moment—things that African Americans were experiencing, especially African American women. Faith took what she had learned in school and combined it with discoveries she had made about African art.

The American People Series #15: Hide Little Children, by Faith Ringgold. 1964, oil on canvas, 36 x 32 in. Private Collection. Photograph courtesy Faith Ringgold.

Ibo mask, Nigeria. Wood. Private Collection. Photograph © The Bridgeman Art Library.

Faith studied and copied patterns, shapes, rhythms, and colors used in African art. She also became inspired by great African American artists like Jacob Lawrence. She began to add these ideas to her paintings.

Ironers, by Jacob Lawrence. 1943, gouache on paper, 21 1/2 x 29 1/2 in. Private Collection. Photograph © The Jacob and Gwendolyn Lawrence Foundation/Art Resource, NY.

Faith was beginning to feel good about her art discoveries. Now she had to find a way to get her paintings noticed more. In the 1960s, people who owned galleries or ran art museums didn't think anyone cared about artwork done by black women. Faith definitely didn't agree. She began showing her work to art dealers all over New York City.

The American People Series #18: The Flag is Bleeding, by Faith Ringgold. 1967, oil on canvas, 72 x 96 in. Collection of the Artist. Photo by Gamma One.

She even helped organize protests in front of New York City art museums when they ignored black artists. The protests helped get museum people interested in African American artists.

Over time, Faith Ringgold and her work began to get noticed, too. By 1973, Faith was selling enough paintings to be able to follow her dream of becoming a full-time artist.

Shakyamuni Buddha and Scenes from His Life, Tibetan tanka. c.1800s, colors and gold on cotton, silk mounts, 27 in. high. Collection of the Newark Museum, Newark, New Jersey. Photograph © The Newark Museum/Art Resource, NY.

Faith discovered something while on a trip to Europe that made it easier for her to show her work around. She saw an exhibition of ancient paintings from Tibet that were framed in cloth. These Tibetan cloth frames are called *tankas*. Faith thought tankas would look great with her paintings.

Now Faith could forget about heavy wooden frames and glass. Tankas allowed her to fold or roll up her paintings. This made it much easier and less expensive to ship her work to galleries and art shows.

Mr. Black Man: The Feminist Series #18, by Faith Ringgold. 1972, acrylic on canvas tanka with printed, pieced, and embroidered fabric, 56 x 26 1/2 in. Collection of the Artist. Photograph courtesy Faith Ringgold.

Faith's mother, Willi, sometimes helped her daughter make tankas. Willi was perfect for the job. She had become a well-known fashion designer in Harlem, and really knew how to sew. Faith had loved sewing from the time she was a little girl. It wasn't long before Faith was using her sewing skills to create her famous quilts.

Faith and her mother Willi working on the quilt *Echoes of Harlem*
Photograph courtesy Faith Ringgold.

Echoes of Harlem, by Faith Ringgold. 1980, acrylic on canvas, dyed, painted and pieced fabric, 96 x 84 in. Phillip Morris Companies, Inc. Photograph courtesy Faith Ringgold.

Quilt making is an African American tradition. In the 1800s, slave women would make quilts for their owners. They often added colorful shapes and designs that came from their African past.

Faith loved writing stories to go along with her quilt paintings. Writing was just about as important to Faith as painting and sculpting.

It's much better to see a real Faith Ringgold quilt than a picture of one. It's interesting to see how she stitched pieces of painted canvas together and made her colorful cloth frames.

It's fun to read the stories on the quilts, too. If you can't find a real Faith Ringgold story quilt to look at, you can check out her many beautifully illustrated children's books. A great example is her first book, *Tar Beach*. It tells the story of Cassie Lightfoot, the main character from the *Tar Beach* story quilts.

The French Collection #1: Dancing at the Louvre, by Faith Ringgold. 1991, acrylic on canvas, tie-dyed, pieced fabric border, 73 1/2 x 80 in. Private Collection. Photograph courtesy Faith Ringgold.

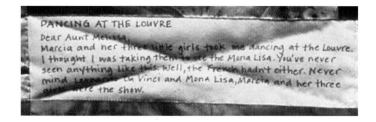

DANCING AT THE LOUVRE
Dear Aunt Melissa,
Marcia and her three little girls took me dancing at the Louvre. I thought I was taking them to see the Mona Lisa. You've never seen anything like this. Well, the French hadn't either. Never mind Leonardo Da Vinci and Mona Lisa, Marcia and her three girls were the show.

Detail of handwritten story from *Dancing at the Louvre.*

Faith also used her knowledge of African art when she created her mask series and soft sculptures. Once again, Faith combined African designs, fabric, and beads to create remarkable three-dimensional works.

Kuba mask, Congo. Wood, raffia, cowrie shells, and beads. Royal Museum for Central Africa, Tervuren, Belgium. Photograph © The Bridgeman Art Library.

Women's Liberation Talking Mask, Witch Mask Series #1, by Faith Ringgold. 1973, mixed media with beads, raffia, cloth, and gourds.
Collection of the Artist. Photograph courtesy Faith Ringgold.

Mrs. Jones and Family, from *Family of Woman Mask Series*, by Faith Ringgold. 1973, sewn fabric and embroidery. Collection of the Artist. Photograph courtesy Faith Ringgold.

Detail from *Cassie and Be Be on Tar Beach*, 2006, glass mosaic installed on the façade of Faith Ringgold's house in New Jersey. 5 x 18 ft. Photograph courtesy Faith Ringgold.

Faith Ringgold has worked hard to make her dream of becoming a full-time artist come true. Today her artwork can be seen in museums and on walls of public buildings all over the United States. Faith has proven in her own life that if someone really, really wants to do something, they can. She believes that just like Cassie Lightfoot, the little girl in the *Tar Beach* story, "anyone can fly."

Works of art in this book can be seen at the following places:

ACA Galleries, New York

The Louvre, Paris

Nationalgalerie, Museum Berggruen, State Museum of Berlin, Germany

Newark Museum, Newark

Royal Museum for Central Africa, Tervuren, Belgium

Solomon R. Guggenheim Museum, New York

Van Gogh Museum, Amsterdam